INHALT

The big wide world   2

Unit **1**   **Teen America**   3

Unit **2**   **Looking ahead**   15

Portfolio Pages   27

Unit **3**   **A Land Down Under**   31

Unit **4**   **Under pressure**   43

Exam Tips   54

●   Diese Aufgabe ist schwieriger.

►S.7   Diese Aufgabe kann nach der Erarbeitung der Schülerbuchseite 7 gemacht werden.

   Eine Aufgabe, die du in dein Heft oder auf Papier schreiben sollst.

   Diese Aufgabe löst du mit dem Hörtext auf der Audio-CD in deinem *Workbook*,
⊙8   Track 8. (Manche Aufnahmen auf der Workbook-Audio-CD sind Texte oder
Textabschnitte aus dem Schülerbuch, die du ohne Aufgaben anhören kannst,
z. B. Track 7 oder Track 16.)
Die *Listening*-Übungen auf S. 6, 19, 36, 47, 52 und 53 können nur mit der
Workbook-Audio-CD gelöst werden. Diese *Listenings* sind nicht Bestandteile der
Schülerbuch-Audio-CD. Die *Tapescripts* zu diesen Aufgaben finden Sie in den
Handreichungen für den Unterricht.

TP   Test Practice: Aufgabentyp entspricht Prüfungsformaten der meisten Bundesländer

---

Hier findest du Hilfen, um die englischen Arbeitsanweisungen zu verstehen.

Circle the word.	**Kreise** das Wort **ein.**
Colour the words **in yellow.**	**Markiere** die Wörter **mit einem gelben Stift.**
Complete ...	**Vervollständige** ...
Cross ... **out.**	**Streiche** ... **durch.**
Crossword (across/down)	**Kreuzworträtsel (waagerecht/senkrecht)**
Invent three dialogues.	**Erfinde** drei Dialoge.
Put ticks (✔) in the table. / Tick ...	**Setze Häkchen in die Tabelle. / Mache Häkchen bei** ...
Which sentence best describes the picture?	**Welcher Satz beschreibt das Bild am besten?**

The big wide world

1 How can you travel? Find eight words in the puzzle (→, ↓, ↘).
Write them next to the right pictures.

1 by *car*

2 by *kayak*

3 by *in-line skates*

4 by *bike*

5 by *motorbike*

6 by *train*

7 by *bus*

8 on *foot*

I	E	H	C	A	R	V	M	F	O	P	Q
A	N	D	R	E	R	J	K	S	O	P	L
J	E	L	A	Q	U	Z	N	I	W	O	M
U	N	L	I	C	D	B	K	Y	T	W	T
G	M	N	L	N	Z	A	A	E	R	B	U
A	B	G	D	E	E	C	Y	P	A	J	Y
Q	Z	D	X	D	I	S	A	Y	I	U	B
K	V	B	I	K	E	Q	K	H	N	I	U
E	U	Y	Z	X	G	D	J	A	L	O	S
L	P	R	U	T	R	W	Y	N	T	K	X
I	M	M	O	T	O	R	B	I	K	E	F
C	V	B	A	T	E	R	M	L	P	Y	S

▶ S. 6

2 Which countries and nationalities are these? Write the missing letters and words.

	country	nationality	capital
	Germany	German	Berlin
	I re _ l an _ d	I rish	Dublin
	S cot _ l an _ d	Scottish	Edinburgh
	A us _ t rali _ a	Australian	Canberra
	Tur _ k e _ y	Turkish	Ankara

▶ S. 7

3 **a)** Write the dialogue in your exercise book.

PARTNER A What languages do you speak?
PARTNER B *My first language is Turkish, but I ... too.*

PARTNER A	PARTNER B
What languages do you speak?	*first language / Turkish / speak / German and English / too.*
Where do you work?	*work / hotel / Berlin*
Do you use your languages at work?	*Yes. / Most of / guests / speak / English*
Have you ever been to America?	*No. / been / Britain.*

b) **Act the dialogue with a partner.**

▶ S. 8

Weitere Übungen zu „The big wide world" findest du auf der CD-ROM.

Unit 1
Teen America

1 Copy this network in your exercise book. How many more words can you find? Write them.

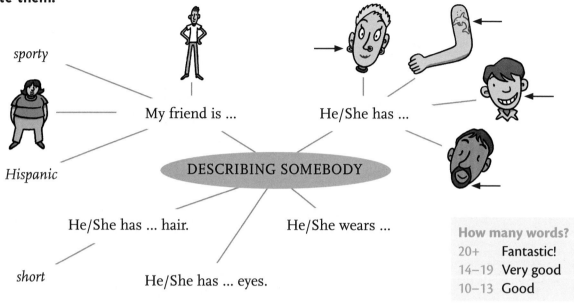

sporty

My friend is ...   He/She has ...

Hispanic

DESCRIBING SOMEBODY

He/She has ... hair.   He/She wears ...

short   He/She has ... eyes.

How many words?
20+   Fantastic!
14–19   Very good
10–13   Good

▶ S. 12

3

three

2 **a)** Describe a famous person (for example a singer or an actor). Write your sentences on some paper.
– What does he/she look like?
– Write other things about the person too.

He's/She's a famous ... / American. / married. / ...
He/She lives in ... / ...

b) GAME
Who is it? Put the descriptions on the wall. Everybody has to guess who the famous people are. Which description is the best?

▶ S. 12

3 Listen again to the teen survey results. Write the right numbers.

 6

What's the most important thing for you?			
• Being happy	_47_ %		
• Having a house, cars and a good job	38 %	• Being rich and/or being famous	_20_ %
• Looking after my family	_30_ %	• Having my own business	7 %
• Having the career of my dreams	25 %	• Being the boss	5 %

▶ S. 13

4 WORDPOWER
What do these question words mean? Draw lines.

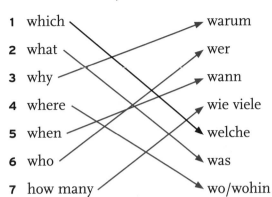

1 which — welche
2 what — was
3 why — warum
4 where — wo/wohin
5 when — wann
6 who — wer
7 how many — wie viele

▶ S. 15

5 How much do you remember about the USA? Try this quiz!

1 How many states are there in the USA?
a) ☐ 40
b) ✔ 50
c) ☐ 60

2 What's the capital of the USA?
a) ☐ New York
b) ☐ Los Angeles
c) ✔ Washington DC

3 Hollywood is part of which city?
a) ☐ New York
b) ✔ Los Angeles
c) ☐ Washington DC

4 Which two states are not near the others?
a) ☐ Hawaii and Texas
b) ✔ Hawaii and Alaska
c) ☐ Hawaii and New Mexico

5 Where is New York?
a) ☐ in the centre
b) ☐ in the west
c) ✔ in the east

6 Who looks after the national parks?
a) ☐ the police
b) ☐ teachers
c) ✔ park rangers

7 What's the biggest city in the USA?
a) ✔ New York
b) ☐ Los Angeles
c) ☐ Washington DC

8 What's the most popular team sport in the USA?
a) ✔ American football
b) ☐ football (soccer)
c) ☐ athletics

▶ S. 15

6 a) Look at the text on page 5.
What do you think the text is about?

a) ☐ young people and tests
b) ✔ young people and drugs in sport
c) ☐ adult sports stars and drugs

Tip:
Before you read a text,
look at the title and pictures.
They help you to guess what
the text is about.

four

4

b) Now read the text quickly.
– Circle all the words you don't know.
– Colour in yellow all the circled words you can guess
(for example, words that are like German words).

Teenagers who use dangerous anabolic steroids[1]

Sport is popular in American schools. A survey of high school students showed that 58 per cent of boys and 51 per cent of girls play sports on a team. Boys' most popular sports are American football, basketball, athletics, baseball and soccer. Girls' favourite sports are basketball, athletics, volleyball, softball and soccer.

5 Sport is good, healthy fun ... isn't it? Many parents are now worried about a report which says that 4 per cent of kids in grades 9 to 12 use anabolic steroids. "Anabolic steroids are illegal drugs that make you faster and stronger – but they are extremely dangerous," says Jim Muir. "Kids need to know how dangerous these drugs are."

Jim knows what he's talking about. He is the father of Tom, 17, who wanted to be in the school baseball 10 team with his friends, but the team coach said that Tom needed to be bigger. Tom started to take anabolic steroids and his weight went up. He was soon picked to play on the team.

But the anabolic steroids had a lot of unhealthy side effects[2]. Tom couldn't sleep at night. He felt ill. He often had headaches[3], his hair started to fall out and he got bad acne. "The worst thing," says his father, "was that his character changed too. He became very aggressive, and his girlfriend left him." 15 One side effect was that Tom became very depressed. Tragically, just before his 18th birthday, Tom tried to kill himself.

Tom's story has a happy ending. His weight is now normal and he doesn't take steroids any more. He plays sport and enjoys himself, but he still has some health problems from the anabolic steroids. "I was lucky," says Tom. "I now do my training without drugs, and I feel good about myself – I work hard 20 and I'm on the baseball team thanks to my own hard work, not the drugs!"

[1] anabolic steroids = *Anabolika*; [2] side effects = *Nebenwirkungen*; [3] headache = *Kopfschmerzen*

5

five

TP **c) Read the text again and tick (✔) the right answer.**

		true	false	not in the text
1	More boys than girls play teams sports in the USA.	✔		
2	Girls don't like playing basketball.		✔	
3	Some kids use drugs because they want to be better at sport.	✔		
4	Tom Muir wanted to lose weight.		✔	
5	Tom was the best player in the baseball team.			✔
6	Steroids can have dangerous side effects.	✔		
7	Tom got steroids from his friends.			✔
8	Tom died because he took drugs.		✔	

● **d) In your exercise book write six side effects that people can get from anabolic steroids.**

They can't sleep at night. They feel/have ... Their ...

► S. 15

TP **7** **Listen to the four conversations. Find the right picture for each conversation.**

Conversation 1 = picture *E*

Conversation 2 = picture *B*

Conversation 3 = picture *D*

Conversation 4 = picture *F*

► S. 16

8 **Listen to some interviews with people in San Francisco, California.**
Tick (✔) the right answers for each person.

A San Francisco food survey		Person 1	Person 2	Person 3	Person 4
1 How often do you eat out in restaurants?	very often		✔		
	sometimes	✔			✔
	never			✔	
2 What kind of food do you like eating?	American	✔		✔	
	European				✔
	Asian		✔		
3 What do you think of fast food?	It's great.			✔	
	It's OK.		✔		
	It's terrible.	✔			✔
4 Do you cook meals at home?	very often	✔			✔
	sometimes		✔		
	never			✔	

► S. 16

9 **a) Finish the phrases in blue.**

1 KEVIN   Are you f*or* or against ready meals?

2 MARY   I'm a*gainst* them. In my o*pinion*, they usually taste terrible!

3 LUIS   I'm not s*ure*. On the one h*and*, I like them, but on the o*ther*

hand h*and*, they're often unhealthy.

4 KEVIN   I t*hink* ready meals are OK. They're good, because they're fast and easy,

but I don't t*hink* they're cheap.

b) AND YOU?
What do you think of ready meals? Give your opinion.

> **Tip:**
> You can use the blue phrases to give or ask for opinions.

▸ S. 17

10 **a) Read the comments. Are they *for* or *against* the topics in the questions?**
Write F *(for)* or A *(against)*.

1 For or against piercings?

a They're really cool. *F*

b They hurt when you get them. *A*

c They make you look different from other

people. *F/A*

2 For or against zoos?

a The animals look sad and depressed. *A*

b It's good that people in cities can see lots

of different animals. *F*

c Wild animals should be free. *A*

3 For or against designer clothes?

a They look great. *F*

b They're too expensive. *A*

c They're great if you want to look cool. *F*

4 For or against cycling?

a It's dangerous if there are fast cars. *A*

b It's no fun when it rains. *A*

c It's better for the environment. *F*

b) AND YOU?
Write each question and your opinion in your exercise book.
Use the phrases in blue from exercise 9a).

> *Are you for or against piercings?*
> *— I'm for piercings, they're cool.*
> *— I'm against piercings. In my opinion, ...*

▸ S. 17

Weitere Übungen zu „Unit 1, Writing" findest du auf der CD-ROM.

11 WORDPOWER
Write the right feelings in English in the crossword.

Across →

1 verlegen

3 enttäuscht

5 erleichtert

7 elend

9 gestresst

10 verblüfft

Down ↓

2 verärgert

4 überrascht

6 aufgeregt

8 gelangweilt

				2				
1 E	M	B	A	R	R	A	S	S	E	D
	4 S			A	N			
3 D	I	S	A	P	P	O	I	N	T	E	D
	U				O			
	R				Y		**6**	
	P	**5** R	E	L	I	E	V	E	D
	R		O		T	D		X	
	I			**8**			C	
7 M	I	S	E	R	A	B	L	E	I
	E			O			T	
	D	**9** S	T	R	E	S	S	E	D
			E			D	
10 P	U	Z	Z	L	E	D	

► S. 18

12 ROLE PLAY
What was it like?
Write the three dialogues in your exercise book. Then practise them with your partner.
Invent three more short dialogues and write them in your exercise book.

A What was your holiday like?

B I was really – it rained all week and I was so !

I was really miserable – it rained all week and I was so bored!

A What was the concert like?

B Well, I was so before it started, but then I was ,
because the band was really bad.

A What were your tests like?

B They were hard! I was really .
I was so when they were over!

 bored

 disappointed

 embarrased

 excited

 miserable

 relieved

 stressed

 surprised

► S. 19

13 Ryan went to the school prom last night. His brother is asking him about it.
Put the sentences in the right order (1–8).
Then write the dialogue in your exercise book.

8	No you can't!!
3	What's she like?
1	What was the school prom like, Ryan?
4	Well, she's friendly and really funny. Her name is Amy.
6	Yes, she has long black hair and a nice smile. I'm seeing her again tomorrow.
2	Awesome! I really enjoyed myself! I danced with a really nice girl all evening.
5	Is she good-looking, this Amy?
7	Can I come too?

▶ S. 19

TP **14** INTERPRETING
Your school is having a party for a group of American exchange students.
You and your friend Finn are talking to Katy, an American girl.

FINN   Schau mal meinen Bruder an. Er hat viel Spaß!

YOU   *Look at Finn's brother. He's* _really enjoying himself!_

KATY   I'm not surprised – he's dancing with Lena.

YOU   *Das* _überrascht sie nicht – er tanzt mit Lena._

FINN   Ja, Lena sieht toll aus. Aber sehr freundlich ist sie nicht.

YOU   _Yes, Lena is really good-looking._

But she isn't very friendly.

KATY   I've never spoken to Lena.

YOU   _Sie hat noch nie mit Lena geredet._

FINN   Sie sitzt neben mir in der Klasse, aber sie redet nicht mit mir.

YOU   _She sits next to Finn in class,_

but she doesn't speak to him.

▶ S. 19

Weitere Übungen zu „Unit 1, Speaking" findest du auf der CD-ROM.

PRACTICE

15 **Reflexive pronouns. Read this advert. Put in the right words.**

→ himself · myself · ourselves · themselves · yourself

Do you cook for *yourself*?

When people don't have much time, they often buy

themselves fast food – but is it healthy?

"No it isn't!" says TV doctor, Dr Tim Green. "In this country,

we are slowly killing *ourselves* with bad food! It's terrible!".

Dr Green says he can make *himself* a healthy meal in only

10 minutes. "I look after *myself* and eat good food.

Buy my new book *Good Food* (only $29.99!) – and change your life!"

Our expert:
Dr Tim Green

►S. 24

16 **Write the missing reflexive pronouns in the table.**

I	*myself*	we	*ourselves*
you	*yourself*	you	*yourselves*
he	*himself*	they	*themselves*
she	*herself*		
it	*itself*		

►S. 24

17 **Read these letters from a magazine's problem page.**
Put in the missing reflexive pronouns. Exercise 16 can help you.

Ask Susi!
Susi helps with all your problems.

Dear Susi,
When we go out, my boyfriend always looks at *himself*
in shop windows and mirrors. He thinks he's so wonderful!
Jo

Jo,
Some people look at *themselves* in mirrors
because they aren't very confident. Tell your boyfriend
he looks great!

Hi Susi,
My sister doesn't look after *herself*.
She's overweight and depressed. What can I do?
Rona

Rona,
My sister and I go jogging and dancing together.

It's healthy and we really enjoy *ourselves* too!

Go out with her and enjoy *yourselves* together!

►S. 24

18 a) Put the time words in the green box into the word web.

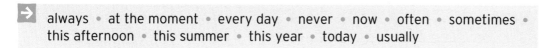

→ always • at the moment • every day • never • now • often • sometimes • this afternoon • this summer • this year • today • usually

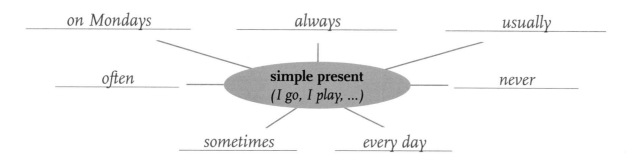

on Mondays   always   usually

often   **simple present** *(I go, I play, ...)*   never

sometimes   every day

at the moment   now   today

this year   **present progressive** *(I'm going, I'm playing, ...)*   this summer

this afternoon

▶ S. 70

b) Simple present or present progressive?
Read the sentences and cross out (= streiche ... durch) **the wrong form of the verb.**
The time words in blue can help you.

Hi Diego!

What *are you doing* / ~~do you do~~ this summer? ~~We're often staying~~ / We *often stay* in Washington state, but this year *we're having* / ~~we have~~ a holiday in California. At the moment ~~we stay~~ / *we're staying* at a campground near the beach. ~~We aren't usually going~~ / We *don't* usually *go* camping, but it's great. *I'm really enjoying myself* / ~~I really enjoy myself~~ here! ~~We're going~~ / We *go* to the beach every day. It's very hot, so *I'm not sitting* / ~~I don't sit~~ in the sun this afternoon.

See you soon, Isaac

▶ S. 70

● 19 Simple present or present progressive?
Read the phone conversation and write the verbs in the right form.

RYAN   Hi Julio, it's Ryan. What (1) *are you doing* _____ *(you/do)* this evening?

JULIO   (2) *I'm not doing* _____ *(I/not/do)* anything special –

       (3) *I'm watching* _____ *(I/watch)* TV.

RYAN   (4) *I usually go* _____ *(I/usually/go)* dancing on Fridays. Do you want to come?

▶ S. 70

20 PRONUNCIATION

a) Do these words sound the same or different? Tick (✔) the right box.

	same (they rhyme)	different (they don't rhyme)
1 *do – too*	✔	
2 bread – said	✔	
3 love – move		✔
4 farm – warm		✔
5 weigh – say	✔	
6 meal – feel	✔	
7 still – I'll		✔
8 more – four	✔	
9 to – so		✔

Tip:
When you learn a new word, learn the pronunciation too! Practise saying the word.

Try saying this tongue twister really fast!

Red lorry, yellow lorry
Red lorry, yellow lorry
Red lorry, yellow lorry ...

b) Write four more examples for your partner. Circle the word that doesn't rhyme with the others.

Sue   come   done   (home)   mum

1 two	you	true	(know)	flew
2 no	grow	(now)	go	yellow
3 date	eight	wait	great	(height)
4 (throw)	shoe	blue	new	threw
5 try	I	my	(happy)	eye

21 Practise saying these sentences. Start with short phrases.

Tip:
If a long sentence is difficult to say, practise it in short phrases.

is Hispanic
my friend is Hispanic
really good-looking

My friend is Hispanic and really good-looking.

1 My friend is Hispanic and really good-looking.

2 He has short black hair and big brown eyes.

3 He's very sporty and plays basketball every week.

4 He sometimes wears a baseball cap and sunglasses.

5 He has a tattoo of a bird on his left arm.

22 **What you can do.**
a) Elizabeth is talking about herself. Read what she says.
Which words mean the same as (= *wie*) **the words in blue? Draw lines.**

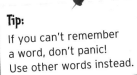
Tip:
If you can't remember
a word, don't panic!
Use other words instead.

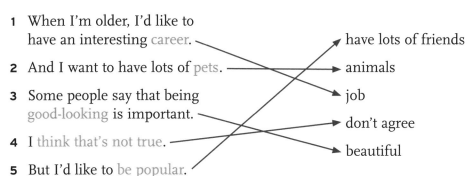

1 When I'm older, I'd like to
  have an interesting career.

2 And I want to have lots of pets.

3 Some people say that being
  good-looking is important.

4 I think that's not true.

5 But I'd like to be popular.

have lots of friends

animals

job

don't agree

beautiful

b) Asif and Bob are talking. Find other words for the phrases in blue.

ASIF My Welsh friend came last weekend. ➜ My friend *from Wales*_____ came last weekend.

BOB On Saturday, we went to the cinema. ➜ On Saturday, we *saw a film*_____.

   – Did you enjoy yourselves? ➜ *Was it fun/good*_____?

ASIF No, the film was boring! ➜ No, the film *wasn't (very) interesting*_____.

BOB The weather was wet on Sunday, wasn't it. ➜ *It rained*_____ on Sunday, didn't it.

ASIF Yes. We didn't go anywhere. ➜ Yes. We *stayed at home*_____.

23 **a) An American girl is staying with Dirk.**
She doesn't speak German.
Can you guess the words Dirk has forgotten?

Tip:
If you can't remember a word, you could
give a description instead! For example:
I'd like a ... you know ... bread and cheese.
– A cheese sandwich?
Yes! I'd like a cheese sandwich.

1 What do you usually have for ... you know ...

  the meal in the morning? *breakfast*_____

2 I usually have bread and a ... you know ... it's a fruit, and it's long and yellow. *banana*_____

3 To drink, I usually have ... um ... it's hot but it isn't coffee. *tea*_____

4 We always eat in the ... um ... the room where you cook. *kitchen*_____

b) You've forgotten the words in blue. Write a description instead.

1 milk – Would you like some ... you know ... it's *a drink and it's white*_____?

2 a ham sandwich – I've made you ... um ... *bread and ham*_____.

3 grandma – This is my ... you know ... *my dad's/mum's mother*_____.

TP 24 ROLE PLAY

a) Read the prompt cards for dialogue 1. Write the questions. Then write the answers.

b) Do the same for dialogue 2.

c) Read dialogues 1 and 2 with your partner.

> **Tip:**
> Use other words if you can't remember a word: For example say *it's near ...* if you can't remember the word *opposite*.

Dialogue 1

Partner A

Your questions:

- When open?

  When is the _cafe open?_

- Where?

  Where is it?

- Hamburgers – how much?

  How much are the hamburgers?

Partner B

> post office
> Bridge Street
> Bob's Burgers
>
> Open Tues – Sun, 10 a.m. – 6 p.m.
> # Bob's Burgers
> Hamburgers only $1.99!
> A new café near you!

Answers: • It's open from _Tuesday to Sunday, 10 a.m. to 6 p.m._

• It's in _Bridge Street, opposite the post office._

• _They're $1.99._

Dialogue 2

Partner A

Your questions:

- When?

  When _is the exercise class?_

- What shoes?

  What shoes do I need?

- Information?

  How can I get information?

Partner B

> and trainers
> sports clothes
> Clothes:
> Phone: 388207
> at Sports Centre
> Wednesday evenings, 7 – 9 p.m.
> Come and join our exercise class!

Answers: • It's _on Wednesday evenings, from 7 to 9 p.m._

• _You need trainers._

• _Phone 388207 for information._

Unit 2
Looking ahead

1 **a)** Look at the pictures and write the jobs 1–9 in the crossword.

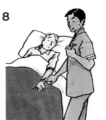

	10									
1	D	A	N	C	E	R				
2	S	C	I	E	N	T	I	S	T	
3 F	L	I	G	H	T	A	T	T	E	N	D	A	N	T
4	F	I	R	E	F	I	G	H	T	E	R
5	S	O	L	D	I	E	R
6 T	R	A	I	N	D	R	I	V	E	R
7	T	E	A	C	H	E	R
8	N	U	R	S	E
9	V	E	T

b) What's the job in number 10?   *astronaut*   ▸ S. 27

▸ S. 27

2 Plans for the future: Read the phrases and write the sentences.

1 | to start | business | my | hope | own | I |

   I hope to start my own business.

2 | months | for | plan | I | six | to go | away |

   I plan to go away for six months.

3 | thinking of | I'm | apprenticeship | doing | an |

   I'm thinking of doing an apprenticeship.

4 | I'm | to do | don't know | I | what | going |

   I don't know what I'm going to do.

▸ S. 27

3 Write five sentences about your plans for the next school holidays. Use these phrases:

*I plan to ... / I hope to ... /
I'm going to ... / I'm thinking of going/starting ...*

Ideas:

go • stay • earn • work •
travel • visit • help

▸ S. 27

Richard Hammond – a Lucky Man!

If you're British and you're a big fan of cars, then you're sure to know Richard Hammond! Richard is a TV presenter on the popular programme "Top Gear" – a programme all about cars. Fast cars.

Richard is lucky – it's his dream job. He's absolutely mad about cars: classic old cars, new cars and, especially, fast cars. He has lots of them, including a Porsche 911, a Dodge Charger, two Land Rovers, a Morgan V6 Roadster, a Ford Mustang GT 390 and a 1963 Opel Kadett – and motor bikes too, for example a Ducati 1098, a Suzuki GSX-R1000 and a Harley Davidson!

Richard Hammond was born on 19th December 1969 in Solihull, a big town in the industrial West Midlands region of England, and two of his grandparents worked in the automobile industry there.

Cars are Richard's hobby and his work, but he has other interests too. He is mad about animals and has four dogs, two cats, three horses, a rabbit and lots of chickens at his home in the country where he lives with his wife and two daughters. Richard is also keen on music, and he plays the bass guitar.

Hammond has been presenting "Top Gear" with Jeremy Clarkson and James May since 2002. At 1.70 m, he is smaller than his co-presenters (Jeremy Clarkson is 1.96 m!), so his nickname is "Hamster". The TV programme is fun, and the presenters always joke with each other. They love making the programmes because they get the chance to drive fantastic, expensive sports cars.

But on 20th September 2006, Richard's career nearly came to a tragic end. Richard had a terrible accident: the car that he was driving, a Vampire Drag car, crashed at the speed of 464 km/h. Richard woke up in hospital. He had very bad head injuries. Even now, Richard says that he still has problems: he forgets lots of things and he has psychological problems. But doctors told him that he nearly died in the crash. One thing he knows: he's very, very lucky!

---

4 **Read the text quickly. What kind of text is it? Tick the right answer.**

A ☐ an article about programmes that are on TV this week

B ☐ a sports report from a newspaper

C ☑ an article about somebody on TV

D ☐ an article about a new film at the cinema

Tip:
Don't worry if you don't understand every word of a text – you can still enjoy reading it.

▶ S. 29

5 **TRAINING Dictionary definitions**
Sometimes a dictionary gives two meanings.
Find these words in the text. Tick the right meaning in this context.

1 **presenter** *(line 2)* = ☑ Moderator ☐ Überbringer

2 **mad** *(line 4)* = ☐ verrückt ☑ **mad about** wild auf / scharf auf

3 **rabbit** *(line 12)* = ☑ Kaninchen ☐ **rabbit on** sülzen

4 **chicken** *(line 12)* = ☑ Huhn ☐ Angsthase

5 **crash** *(line 20)* = ☐ krachen ☑ einen Unfall haben

▶ S. 29

6 TRAINING Without a dictionary
Find these words. Guess the meanings.
How did you guess? Put ticks (✔) in the table.
(You can put more than one tick.)

Tip:
You don't always need a dictionary!
You can often guess a word if ...
– you know part of the word or phrase.
– you can guess from the context.
– it looks like a German word.

English	I know part of the word/phrase	I can guess from the context	It looks like a German word	German
line 5 classic			✔	klassisch
line 9 industrial	✔		✔	industriell
line 13 bass guitar	✔		✔	Bassgitarre
line 15 nickname	✔	✔		Spitzname
line 17 sports car	✔	✔		Sportwagen
line 19 tragic		✔	✔	tragisch
line 23 psychological			✔	psychologisch

►S. 29

7 Read the text again. Write the information in the table.

name	Richard Hammond
nickname	hamster
job	TV presenter
date of birth	19th December 1969
place of birth	Solihull
children	two daughters
pets	dogs, cats, horses, a rabbit, chickens
musical instrument	bass guitar
● Give two reasons why he's lucky.	He has his dream job. He didn't die in the accident.

►S. 29

8 Write your opinion about each job (1–5).

Would you like to be ...
1 a firefighter?
2 a shop assistant?
3 an actor?
4 a vet?
5 a train driver?

Ideas:
The pay is good/bad.
I'd like / I wouldn't like to be famous.
You need / You don't need special training.
It's interesting/boring/hard/easy/fun/exciting/(too) dangerous.
I like / I don't like animals/trains.

Tip:
Use opinion phrases from Unit 1:
I'm not sure.
On the one hand ...,
but on the other hand ...
In my opinion, ...
I think the job is ... because ...

1) I wouldn't like to be a firefighter. In my opinion, it's too dangerous.
I'm not sure. On the one hand, it's exciting, but on the other hand, ...

▶ S. 32

18

eighteen

9 What can you see in the picture? Write one sentence or more for each question.

1 How many people are there in the picture?

2 Where are they?

3 What can you buy there?

4 What does the shop assistant look like?

5 What are the two boys interested in?

6 What's the girl going to do?

7 What's the woman doing?

8 What has she bought?

▶ S. 32

Tip:
Underline the verbs in the questions.
Use the right forms of the verbs in
your answers.

TP **10** **WORDPOWER**
a) Write the missing headings in this form.

→ Address • details
Education • E-mail
experience • First
Hobbies • Mobile
Surname

• **Personal** *details*

Surname : Harris

First names: Sophie ~~Jane~~ *Anna*

Address : 16 ~~Plum~~ Road, Hull HU6 4JH *Park*

Mobile number: 07946 ~~129~~ 032 *127*

E-mail address: Sophie~~52~~@fast.com *25*

• *Education*

Millbank Secondary School

• **Work** *experience*

Saturday job in a ~~coffee~~ shop *sports*

• *Hobbies*

In-line skating, kayaking and ~~reading~~ *dancing*

b) Now listen to the interview. Correct the mistakes in the form.

► S. 35

⊚ 13

TP **11** Look at each picture and listen to three sentences: A, B and C.
Which sentence best describes the picture? Tick A, B or C.

⊚ 14

1

A ☐ B ✔ C ☐

2

A ☐ B ✔ C ☐

3

A ☐ B ☐ C ✔

4

A ✔ B ☐ C ☐

5

A ☐ B ☐ C ✔

6

A ☐ B ✔ C ☐

► S. 35

SPEAKING

12 WORDPOWER

Try to write a job for each letter of the alphabet! How many jobs can you find?

astronaut, babysitter, cook, d...

Then compare with your partner – can you make a longer list together?

▶ S. 36

13 a) Write two questions for each verb (1–6).

You can use different words too.

1 **wear** ... a uniform / special clothes / a suit

2 **help** ... people / animals / ill children

3 **work** ... indoors / outdoors / with children

4 **use** ... special equipment / machines / a computer

5 **earn** ... lots of money / good pay

6 **work** ... at weekends / in a factory / in an office / with your hands

Do you wear a uniform?
Do you wear a suit?

b) ROLE PLAY   What's my job?
Partner B chooses a job.
Partner A asks questions and tries to guess Partner B's job.
How many questions do you need?
Now play again – Partner A chooses a job.

Tip:
Use questions from a).

PARTNER A

PARTNER B

Do you work with children?

No, I don't.

Do you work outdoors?

Sometimes.

Do you help animals?

Yes, I do.

Are you a vet?

Yes, I am. Well done – that was only four questions!

▶ S. 36

20

twenty

TP 14 **INTERPRETING**

Your British friend, Rob, is staying with you.
Your mum wants to ask about Rob's parents,
but she doesn't speak English.
Can you help?

MUM Wo arbeitet dein Vater, Rob?

YOU *Where does your dad work, Rob?*

_____

ROB He has his own business. He's a plumber.

YOU *Er hat seine eigene Firma. Er ist Klempner.*

MUM Hat deine Mutter eine Arbeitstelle?

YOU *Does your mum have a job?*

ROB No. She worked in a boutique, but it closed, so now she's unemployed.

YOU *Nein. Sie hat mal in einer Boutique gearbeitet, aber der Laden hat geschlossen,*

also ist sie nun arbeitslos.

MUM Das ist schlimm. Ich war letztes Jahr auch arbeitslos. Jetzt arbeite ich in einer Fabrik.

YOU *That's bad. Last year I was unemployed too. Now I work in a factory.*

▸ S. 37

15 **MEDIATING**

Rob wants to know what this magazine article
is about. Write the main points in English.

Tip:
You don't have to translate every word.
Just write the main points.

Du brauchst Geld oder möchtest dein Taschengeld aufbessern?
Gründe deine eigene kleine Firma!

Hier ein paar Ideen:

- **Tiersitten**: Wenn deine Nachbarn in Urlaub fahren, könntest du dich um ihre Tiere kümmern.
  Und deine Preise sind bestimmt günstiger als im Tierheim oder in einer Tierpension.

- **Kuchenbacken**: Wie wäre es mit einem Kuchenstand an deiner Schule?
  Du backst zwei oder drei Kuchen und verkaufst sie in der Pause.

- **Putzen**: Biete einen Putzdienst für Nachbarn oder Freunde deiner Eltern.
  Wenn du deinen MP3-Player an hast, ist es gar nicht so langweilig.

- **Einkaufsservice**: Du könntest für andere einkaufen gehen – z. B. für ältere Nachbarn oder Leute,
  die wenig Zeit haben.

It's an article about how to earn some money. Some ideas are:
– when your neighbours go on holiday, look after their animals.
– make ...

▸ S. 37

16 a) If-sentences (type II). Circle the right form of the verbs.

QUIZ! Are you a lion or a mouse ?

1 What would you do if you saw a ghost?

☐ **A** I'd (shout)/ shouted "HELP!!!"

☐ **B** I'd talked /(talk) to it.

2 What would you do if you had to sing in a concert?

☐ **A** I'd saying /(say) I was ill and I (wouldn't go)/ didn't go.

☐ **B** I'd loved /(love) every minute of it.

3 What would you do if you were at the top of the Empire State Building?

☐ **A** I'd (close)/ closing my eyes.

☐ **B** I'd took /(take) lots of photos.

22

twenty-two

b) Now do the quiz! Answers: More As: Oh dear – you're a mouse • More Bs: Congratulations! You're a lion!

▶ S. 38

17 Helen is thinking about the summer.
Finish the sentences. The verbs after *If I ...* should be in the simple past.

1 If I looked in the newspaper, I'd **find** a summer job.

2 *If I found* a job, I'd **work** all summer.

3 *If I worked*_____ all summer, I'd **earn** lots of money.

4 *If I earned*_____ lots of money, I'd **go** on holiday.

5 *If I went*_____ on holiday, I'd **visit** the USA.

6 *If I visited*_____ the USA, I'd **stay** there for six weeks.

7 *If I stayed*_____ there for six weeks, I'd **have** no time for a job.

8 *If I had*_____ no time for a job, I wouldn't earn any money – and I wouldn't go on holiday!

▶ S. 38

• 18 What would you do if you won 50,000 euros? Write five sentences.

→ go to • buy • visit • give • save • spend

If I won 50,000 euros, I'd ...

▶ S. 38

REVISION

19 **Past tenses**
Marilyn Lowe works as a police detective. There was a bank robbery
(= Raub) **this morning. She's asking a neighbour some questions.
Underline the verb phrases in the simple past. Circle the verb
phrases in the past progressive.**

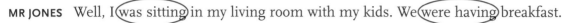

DETECTIVE   Mr Jones, your flat is above the bank. What were you doing
at the time of the robbery? <u>Did you see</u> anything?

MR JONES   Well, I was sitting in my living room with my kids. We were having breakfast.

DETECTIVE   <u>Did you hear</u> any noises?

MR JONES   No, we <u>didn't hear</u> anything, I'm sure about that. Some children were playing loudly in
the garden when I <u>started</u> my breakfast and they were still shouting when I <u>finished</u>.

▶ S. 76

20 **Read Detective Lowe's second interview.
Put the verbs in the right forms – simple past or past progressive.**

DETECTIVE   Mrs Mack, what *(you/do)* _were you doing_____ when *(the robbery/happen)*

_the robbery happened?_____

MRS MACK   *(I/work)* _I was working_____ in front of my shop, opposite the bank.

DETECTIVE   *(you/see)* _Did you see_____ anything?

MRS MACK   Well, *(I/see)* _I saw_____ two men. *(They/stand)* _They were standing_____
near the bank. *(One man/talk)* _One man was talking_____ on his mobile.

DETECTIVE   What *(he/say)* _was he saying_____?

MRS MACK   Sorry – *(I/not hear)* _I didn't hear_____. Then *(a car/arrive)* _a car arrived_____
and *(the men/get in)* _the men got in_____.

▶ S. 76

● **21** **Write the end of the interview.**

DETECTIVE   when / car / come?

MRS MACK   it / come / about 9.15 a.m.

DETECTIVE   you / see / who / drive / car?

MRS MACK   yes, / man / wear / big hat.

DETECTIVE   where / car / stop?

MRS MACK   it / stop / outside / bank. One man / wait / in car /
while / other men / steal / money in bank.

DETECTIVE   when / men / leave / bank?

MRS MACK   I don't know. They / leave / while / I / work / in / shop.

▶ S. 76

TP **22** **What do these signs and posters say?
Tick A, B, C or D.**

Tip:
• Read the signs and the four answers very carefully: some of the answers are nearly the same!
• Tick only *one* answer.
• If you don't know the answer, always guess – never write nothing.

1

*Holston Library &
Learning Centre Cafe*

**SPECIAL OFFER
Buy one coffee,
get one free!**

A ☐ You don't have to pay for coffee at the cafe.

B ☑ You can buy two coffees for the price of one.

C ☐ You have to buy two cups of coffee at the cafe.

D ☐ They're selling special coffee.

---

2 *Holston Library*

**Opening times
Monday to Friday:**
10 a.m. to 9 p.m.
Saturday:
10 a.m. to 5 p.m.
Sunday:
10 a.m. to 2 p.m.

A ☐ The library is open in the evening at weekends.

B ☐ On Tuesdays you can get books between 10 a.m. and 2 p.m. only.

C ☐ The library is not open every day.

D ☑ You can get books between 10 a.m. and 9 p.m. on Wednesdays.

---

3 *LOST!*

(near Newport Rd)
*Brown leather woman's
bag with purse and keys*

*£20 reward if you find it!
Contact Jenny on
077944 401218*

A ☐ Jenny wants to buy a bag.

B ☐ Jenny found £20 near Newport Road.

C ☑ Jenny can't find her bag.

D ☐ Jenny is selling a bag for £20.

---

4 *Holston Library &
Learning Centre*
VOLUNTEERS WANTED

*to help make a garden
for the library*
*Meet every Sunday
in April and May
9.30 a.m. at the front door*

A ☑ You can make a garden for the library for no pay.

B ☐ They're making a garden for the library this autumn.

C ☐ You can get a job in the library cafe.

D ☐ They're going to work on the garden all weekend.

---

5 *Holston Library &
Learning Centre*

Please note: *next week,
the judo class will be on
Tuesday afternoon
(instead of Wednesday)
thank you*

A ☐ You can do judo at the learning centre next Wednesday.

B ☐ There will be a judo class at the learning centre on Tuesday and Wednesday.

C ☐ The learning centre needs a judo teacher.

D ☑ There will be no judo class next Wednesday.

TP **23** **a)** **Read the texts and find each person's hobby.**
(There are more hobbies than people.)

Person	1	2	3	4	5	6
Hobby	*F*	*H*	*A*	*B*	*I*	*D*

Tip:
• You won't find the names of the hobbies in the texts! Look for words that mean the same. For example:
I make pizzas or spaghetti = cooking
• Read all of a sentence – don't just look at the main words. Small words can change the meaning! For example:
"*I **don't** really like classical music*" is the opposite of "*I really like classical music.*"

1

I sometimes watch TV, but I'd rather spend my time with my books and magazines. I love fantasy and adventure stories, especially by the author Philip Pullman.
Mikey

2

I'm terrible at sport, but I like watching it on TV. My friends often come round and I make pizza or spaghetti, or sometimes I make a whole meal for them. I like to experiment and make up my own recipes.
Jo

Hobbies:
the person …
A: sings in a band
B: goes rock-climbing
C: collects stamps
D: is a volunteer at an animal rescue centre
E: does judo
F: reads a lot
G: plays the piano in an orchestra
H: likes cooking
I: plays rugby and basketball

3

I like all sorts of music, especially heavy metal (although I don't really like classical music). I like singing and everyone says I've got a good voice.
Robert

4

I hate team sports, but I love outdoor activities, especially in the country. The fresh air and mountain scenery make me forget all my problems. The worst thing for me is to be stuck indoors in front of the TV.
Hayley

5

I really love animals, but I'm allergic to dogs and cats so we can't have any at home. I'm pretty good at sport, and I enjoy team sports and doing things with other people.
Max

6

I like helping people and animals and I'd like to be a nurse in a care home when I'm older. I've got lots of pets – I'm mad about dogs, cats and horses. I love looking after them all.
Jade

● **b)** **Find words in the texts that mean …**

Remember:
You can often guess a word if …
– you know part of the word or phrase.
– you can guess from the context.
– it looks like a German word.

1 a person who writes books: *author*

2 instructions for cooking things: *recipes*

3 when something makes you ill: *allergic to*

4 a place where people live if they can't look after themselves: *care home*

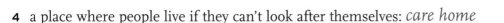

Volunteering is fun!

Hi! I'm Jodie and I'm seventeen. I'm a volunteer at a youth club for people with special needs[1]. Some of the people who come to the club are autistic, some have Down's syndrome or other learning problems, and some are in wheelchairs. They're all young, between fifteen and twenty-five. The club is
5   great fun – we all enjoy going there.

We meet every Thursday evening and do lots of interesting activities. Sometimes we cook things – we've made pizzas and cakes. We usually listen to CDs of our favourite bands, and we have guitars and a keyboard so we can make music ourselves.

10   One day in the summer holidays we all went on a boat trip on the river, which was awesome! We each helped the men to drive the boat.

Last Thursday was a really good night. We all went to a hairdressing salon near the club – they opened the salon in the evening just for us! The hairdressers gave everybody training in hairdressing. They showed us how to wash and dry hair and we practised with a partner. I really enjoyed myself – but I don't think my
15   partner liked her hair when I finished!

For me, the best thing about the club is all the new friends that I've made.

A boy from the club at the boat trip

[1] people with special needs = *Behinderte*

TP 24 Read the article and answer the questions. Write complete sentences.

1   How old are the people who go to the club?

They're between *fifteen and twenty-five*   .

2   When does Jodie go to the club?

She goes every Thursday evening   .

3   What musical instruments do they have?

They have guitars and a keyboard   .

4   What did they do last summer?

They went on a boat trip   .

5   Where did they go last week?

They went to a hairdressing salon   .

6   What did Jodie think of the visit?

She really enjoyed herself   .

● 7   Why wasn't Jodie's partner very happy?

She didn't like her hair   .

● 8   Why does Jodie like the club?

She's made (lots of) new friends   .

> **Tip:**
> Remember to put verbs and other words in the right form in your answers. For example:
> *When does Jodie go ...?*
> → *Jodie goes ...*
> *I enjoyed myself.*
> → *She enjoyed herself.*
> Sometimes you have to change things more. For example:
> *I don't think my partner liked ...*
> → *She didn't like ...*

Hier kannst du darüber nachdenken, was du in den Units 1 und 2 schon alles gelernt hast.

Das kann ich!

Was kannst du **sehr gut** ↑ oder schon **recht gut** → ? Bei welchen Aufgaben musst du dich noch **verbessern** ↓ ? Zeichne die Pfeile ein.

Unit 1

Ich kann jemanden mit mehreren Begriffen beschreiben
(z. B. *She's sporty and has short hair.*).
(Tipp: Schau dir die Übungen 1–2 auf Seite 3 an.) ☐

Ich kann mindestens sechs englische Fragewörter nennen und ich kenne ihre deutsche Bedeutung.
(Tipp: Schau dir die Übung 4 auf Seite 4 an.) ☐

Ich kann meine Meinung über verschiedene Themen mit mindestens drei verschiedenen Redewendungen ausdrücken.
(Tipp: Schau dir die Übungen 9–10 auf Seite 7 an.) ☐

Ich kann Reflexivpronomen (z. B. *myself, yourself*) benutzen.
(Tipp: Schau dir die Übungen 15–17 auf Seite 10 an.) ☐

Ich kann sagen, was ich jetzt (z. B. *I'm reading now.*) und was ich oft mache
(z. B. I *play tennis every week.*).
(Tipp: Schau dir die Übungen 18–19 auf Seite 11 an.) ☐

In mein Portfolio lege ich:

_____

Unit 2

Ich kann über Zukunftspläne reden.
(Tipp: Schau dir die Übung 2 auf Seite 15 an.) ☐

Ich kann meine Meinung über verschiedene Berufe äußern.
(Tipp: Schau dir die Übung 8 auf Seite 18 an.) ☐

Ich kann jemanden zu seinem Beruf befragen (z. B. *Do you …*).
(Tipp: Schau dir die Übung 13 auf Seite 20 an.) ☐

Ich kann in einem einfachen Gespräch zwischen Englisch und Deutsch sprechenden Personen dolmetschen.
(Tipp: Schau dir die Übung 14 auf Seite 21 an.) ☐

Ich kann *if*-Sätze verstehen und selber bilden (z. B. *If I found a job, I'd work all summer.*). ☐
(Tipp: Schau dir die Übungen 16–18 auf Seite 22 an.)

In mein Portfolio lege ich:

_____

Meine Fortschritte in Englisch sind groß ☐ mittel ☐ klein ☐ nicht erkennbar ☐ .

Tipp: Du kannst auch einen Partner / eine Partnerin bzw. deine Lehrerin / deinen Lehrer fragen, was er/sie zu deiner Einschätzung meint.

Weitere Übungen zu „Das kann ich!" findest du auf der CD-ROM.

PORTFOLIO

Das kann ich auch noch!

Ich kenne sechs Adjektive, die Gefühle beschreiben (z. B. *happy, ...*).
(Tipp: Schau dir Seite 18 in deinem Englischbuch an.)

Ich kann sechs verschiedene Berufe nennen (z. B. *teacher, ...*).
(Tipp: Schau dir Seite 27 in deinem Englischbuch an.)

Meine Fertigkeiten im Sprechen und Lesen

Look at the tips on the *Test Training*-pages in Units 1 and 2. Copy three tips each for *Speaking* and *Reading*: two tips that have helped you and one tip that you're going to try.

SPEAKING

These tips helped me:

I'm going to try this tip:

READING

These tips helped me:

I'm going to try this tip:

Hier kannst du darüber nachdenken, was du in den Units 3 und 4 schon alles gelernt hast.

Das kann ich!

Was kannst du **sehr gut** ↑ oder schon **recht gut** →? Bei welchen Aufgaben musst du dich noch **verbessern** ↓? Zeichne die Pfeile ein.

Unit 3

Ich kann beschreiben, was ich auf einem Bild sehe (z. B. Landschaften, Personen und Situationen).
(Tipp: Schau dir die Übung 2 auf Seite 31 und die Übung 18 auf Seite 40 an.)

Ich kann mit einem Partner / einer Partnerin über einen Film sprechen.
(Tipp: Schau dir die Übungen 5–6 auf Seite 34 an.)

Ich kann an ein Hotel schreiben und um Auskünfte für meine Urlaubsplanung bitten (z. B. Lage des Campingplatzes, Zimmerpreise).
(Tipp: Schau dir die Übungen 12–13 auf Seite 37 an.)

Ich kann das Passiv verstehen, bilden und verwenden (z. B. *Kangaroos are found in Australia. The hospital was saved.*).
(Tipp: Schau dir die Übungen 14–15 auf Seite 38 an.)

Ich kann je fünf Sätze mit *going to-future* und *will-future* bilden.
(Tipp: Schau dir die Übungen 16–17 auf Seite 39 an.)

In mein Portfolio lege ich:

Unit 4

Ich kann einen Text über Tätowierungen schreiben und meine Meinung dazu deutlich machen.
(Tipp: Schau dir die Übungen 5–6 auf Seite 46 an.)

Ich kann notieren, was jemand am Telefon gesagt hat.
(Tipp: Schau dir die Übung 8 auf Seite 47 an.)

Ich kann fünf Tätigkeiten im Haushalt nennen, z. B. *cook*.
(Tipp: Schau dir die Übung 9 auf Seite 48 an.)

Ich kann Fragen mit *do, does* und *did* stellen.
(Tipp: Schau dir die Übung 13–15 auf Seite 50 an.)

Ich kann fünf Sätze mit der *ing*-Form schreiben, z. B. *Playing cards is fun, I tried diving.*
(Tipp: Schau dir die Übungen 16–17 auf Seite 51 an.)

In mein Portfolio lege ich:

Meine Fortschritte in Englisch sind groß ☐ mittel ☐ klein ☐ nicht erkennbar ☐ .

Tipp: Du kannst auch einen Partner / eine Partnerin bzw. deine Lehrerin / deinen Lehrer fragen, was er/sie zu deiner Einschätzung meint.

Weitere Übungen zu „Das kann ich!" findest du auf der CD-ROM.

PORTFOLIO

Das kann ich auch noch!

Ich kann sechs Dinge nennen, die man auf einem Bild sehen kann
(z. B. *There's the sea. I can see cows, ...*).
(Tipp: Schau dir Seite 41 in deinem Englischbuch an.)

_____

Ich kann sechs Probleme nennen (z. B. *not enough money, ...*).
(Tipp: Schau dir Seite 55 in deinem Englischbuch an.)

_____

Meine Fertigkeiten im Schreiben und Hören

Look at the tips on the *Test Training*-pages in Units 3 and 4. Copy three tips each for *Writing* and *Listening*: two tips that have helped you and one tip that you're going to try.

WRITING

These tips helped me:

_____

_____

_____

I'm going to try this tip:

_____

_____

LISTENING

These tips helped me:

_____

_____

_____

I'm going to try this tip:

_____

_____

Unit 3
A Land Down Under

TP **1** **Four lives: listen again to the four people. Complete these sentences.**

⊙15

1 Jessica isn't Australian: she's *British* . Her family came to Australia *three/3*

years ago. She misses her grandparents and her *cousins* .

2 Uluru is about *350* metres high. Tom's father is a tour *guide* . He takes

tourists around the rock.

3 Melbourne is in the *south-east* of Australia. In December and January, it can get hot

– up to *40* degrees!

4 Ralph is learning to be an Australian *cowboy* . They use horses and

motorbikes too.

▶ S. 41

2 **a) Describing a picture. Cross out the words you can't use in these sentences.**

1 You can see a cat in the ...   foreground/~~down under~~/background/~~apprenticeship~~/car.

2 On the left, there are some ...   people/animals/~~hours~~/~~perhaps~~/children.

3 The adults are ...   sitting/standing/exciting/talking/~~piercing~~/~~buildings~~.

4 The man on the right has ...   ~~puzzled~~/a beard/a tattoo/~~blonde~~/sunglasses.

5 The woman on the left is ...   good-looking/~~raining~~/slim/~~size~~/pregnant.

6 I think the boy feels ...   ~~multicultural~~/annoyed/~~nationality~~/embarrassed/disappointed.

**b) Now write at least six sentences (● ten sentences) about this picture.
The sentences in 2a) can help you.**

Ideas:
● What can you see?
● What are the children doing?
● What's the man on the left doing?
● What's the woman wearing?
● How does the little girl look?
● What's the weather like?

▶ S. 41

An Exciting Birth

A baby girl was born in a Royal Flying Doctor Service (RFDS) plane in the state of South Australia on Saturday.

5 The baby's father, Glenn Anderson, phoned the hospital in their home town, Mount Gambier, in the middle of Friday night, to tell them the baby was coming – eight weeks early!

10 "We were really worried because we knew it was too early," said Mr Anderson. "The hospital here said we had to go to the big hospital in Adelaide because the baby would need special equipment. It was terrible!" The Andersons live 450 km from the state capital, Adelaide. That's about six hours away: too far to go by road.

15 The Royal Flying Doctor Service was called and a special plane was sent to Mount Gambier. Mrs Jennifer Anderson and her husband were taken to the hospital in Adelaide – but the baby couldn't wait! She was born at 8.30 a.m., just minutes before they arrived in Adelaide, with the help of a nurse on the plane.

"I can't describe how happy we are!" said Mr Anderson. "I'd like to thank all the doctors and nurses at the hospital and the team on the plane – they were absolutely fantastic, and we're so lucky that our baby is safe 20 and healthy. The RFDS saved our baby's life. We've called her Harriet, because that's the name of the nurse on the plane," he added.

Mother and baby are still in hospital. Harriet, who weighed only 1.3 kg at birth, is in an incubator at the moment and will stay in hospital for some time, but doctors say that she is a strong little girl.

3 **a) Read the article. One thing is wrong in each sentence. Cross it out and correct it.**

1 The article is about a baby and the Royal Flying ~~Teacher~~ Service. *Doctor*

2 The baby was born in a ~~shop~~. *plane*

3 Mrs Jennifer Anderson had a baby ~~boy~~ at the weekend. *girl*

4 The baby was eight weeks ~~late~~. *early*

5 Mr and Mrs Anderson live in ~~Adelaide~~, South Australia. *Mount Gambier*

6 Mount Gambier is six ~~days~~ away from Adelaide. *hours*

7 Mr and Mrs Anderson went to Adelaide hospital by ~~car~~. *plane*

8 The baby was born at half-past eight on Saturday ~~evening~~. *morning*

9 They called the baby Harriet because ~~her mother~~ was called Harriet. *the nurse*

10 Mrs Anderson and her baby are ~~now at home~~. *still in hospital*

▶ S. 45

● **b) Find the opposites for these words. You can find them all in the article.**

		opposite
1	died	*was born*
2	north	*south*
3	late	*early*
4	small	*big*
5	near	*far*
6	sad	*happy*
7	fantastic	*terrible*

► S. 45

4 **Read Erin's e-mail and write the right word in each space** (= *Lücke*).

Hi Megan!

Did I tell you I have a new pet (1) *rabbit*　　?

He's white and really friendly and he's called Snowy.

But mum says rabbits are dirty, so I have to

(2) *keep*　　him out of the house.

I'm (3) *allowed*　　to play with him in the garden.

Last week the garden gate was open and Snowy

(4) *escaped*　　! I looked everywhere for him.

I wanted to phone the (5) *police*　　, but mum

said that was silly. I was really (6) *miserable*

without my rabbit and I put posters in all the shops.

At (7) *last*　　somebody phoned and told me

there was a white rabbit in a farm (8) *building*

near our house. I went there and brought him home.

I was so (9) *relieved*　　!

Tip:
Read the text first. Then think about the missing words – which word is right in the context?
If you're not sure, read the sentence again – with each word in it.

1　bike / brother / rabbit / toy
2　behave / give / keep / train
3　against / allowed / annoyed / clever
4　ate / embarrassed / escaped / lost
5　plumber / police / pool / pyjamas
6　beautiful / clever / happy / miserable
7　last / least / once / the moment
8　background / boss / building / bush
9　depressed / relieved / tired / pregnant

► S. 45

5 WORDPOWER
What kind of films are these?
Find the missing letters (a, e, i, o, u) and write the complete words.

1 w*st*rn   *western*

2 c*m*dy   *comedy*

3 thr*ll*r   *thriller*

4 h*rr*r f*lm   *horror film*

5 *ct**n f*lm   *action film*

6 r*m*nc*   *romance*

▸ S. 46

6 ROLE PLAY   Three Australian films

a) Find the right answers to questions 1–6. Draw lines. Then write the dialogue.

PARTNER A

1 What's the title of the film?

2 What kind of film is it?

3 What's it about?

4 What happens in the film?

5 Who's the star of the film?

6 Is it a good film?

PARTNER B

It's about a girl who dreams of a big wedding.

It's a romantic comedy, but it's sad too.

It's *Muriel's Wedding*.

The star is Toni Collette, who plays Muriel.

Yes, it's a great film. It's very funny.

The girl leaves her boring life in a small town and goes to live in Sydney.

b) Practise the dialogue with your partner.

c) Now write dialogues about these two films. Use the questions (1–6) from 6a). Then practise the dialogues with your partner.

- *Walkabout*
- drama *(= spannender Film)*
- white girl, brother and an Aboriginal boy
- girl and boy get lost in bush / meet Aboriginal boy / helps them
- stars: Jenny Agutter and David Gumpilil (plays Aboriginal boy)
- great film, but very sad too

- *Crocodile Dundee*
- comedy
- man from Australian bush
- an American journalist meets Mick (man who lives in bush) / invites him to New York / Mick has never been to a city!
- star: Paul Hogan (plays Mick)
- awesome / really funny

d) Write a dialogue about another film (it needn't be Australian). Then practise the dialogue with your partner.

▸ S. 46

TP **7** INTERPRETING

**Your Australian friend, Jack, is staying with you. Your aunt Lili wants
to ask him about films, but she doesn't speak English. Can you help?**

LILI Wer ist dein Lieblingsschauspieler, Jack?

YOU *Who's your favourite* actor, Jack _____?

JACK David Gulpilil. He's an Aboriginal Australian.
Do you know him?

YOU *David Gulpilil. Er ist australischer Urein-*

wohner. Kennst du ihn?

LILI Nein.

YOU *No(, I don't).*

JACK His first film was *Walkabout*, but he was also in *Crocodile Dundee* and lots of other films.
Before he became an actor, he was a hunter and tracker.

YOU *Sein erster Film war* **Walkabout**, *aber er war auch in* **Crocodile Dundee** *und in*

vielen anderen Filmen. Bevor er Schauspieler wurde, war er Jäger und Fährten-

sucher.

LILI Ich habe *Crocodile Dundee* gesehen, aber *Walkabout* habe ich nicht gesehen.
Den Film würde ich gerne sehen.

YOU *I've seen* **Crocodile Dundee** *but I haven't seen* **Walkabout**. *I'd like to see the film.*

▶ S. 47

8 MEDIATING

**Lili wants to know what this TV programme is about.
Write the main points in German.**

Tip:
Remember: you don't have
to translate every word.
Just write the main points.

7.30 *Documentary: Dame Edna Everage*

Dame Edna Everage is perhaps the most famous woman
in Australia – or should we say *man*? Dame Edna is, of
course, the well-known comedy character played by male
comedian Barry Humphries. Everybody knows what
Dame Edna looks like – her lilac-coloured hair, her large,
fancy glasses, her film-star clothes. Everybody loves her:
she chats, she gives advice, she's friendly – and at the
same time, she makes fun of the celebrities she's talking
to. She's *very* funny.

▶ S. 47

TP **9** **Listen to four news reports on the radio.**
Find the right picture for each report.

Report 1 = Picture *E*   Report 3 = Picture *F*

Report 2 = Picture *B*   Report 4 = Picture *C*

A

B

C

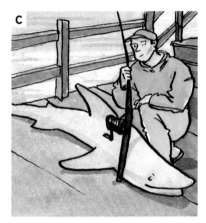

D

E

F

▶ S. 49

TP **10** **Listen to the announcements and write the missing information.**

1

Train: Nerang Station to Brisbane Airport

Leaves from platform number: *3*

Leaves at: *7.15*

Arrives at: *8.50*

2

Brisbane to Cairns:

Flight number: QF 07*86*

Leaves from gate number: *12*

Boarding time: *19.20*

▶ S. 49

TP ● **11** **Listen to the conversation and finish these sentences.**

1 The woman can't find *her boarding pass*   .

2 She finds it in *her book*   .

3 I think the woman feels *stupid/silly/...*   at the end.

▶ S. 49

12 **Complete the questions with the right words from the boxes.**

→ are • can • do (2x) • does • is

1 _Does_ your campground have a pool?

2 _Do_ buses stop near the campground?

3 _Is_ there a cafe?   5 _Can_ we hire tennis equipment?

4 _Are_ there shops in the campground?   6 _Do_ you have a website?

→ how far • how many • how much • what • when • which

7 _When_ do you close for winter?   10 _How far_ is the beach from the campground?

8 _How much_ is it per night?   11 _Which_ station is nearer, Robina or Kerang?

9 _What_ is the nearest town called?   12 _How many_ dogs can we bring?

► S. 51

13 **a) Find useful phrases for an e-mail to a hotel. Draw lines.**

1 Dear ...   ask for some information.

2 I'm coming to ...   faithfully,

3 I'm writing to ...   Sir/Madam,

4 I'm looking forward to ...   Australia with my family.

5 Yours ...   hearing from you.

b) Look at the pictures and read the phrases.
Then write an e-mail to a hotel and ask these questions.

restaurant?

how much / night?

buses?

> **Tip:**
> The questions in 12
> and the phrases in
> 13a) can help you.

near hotel?

how far?

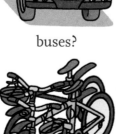
hire bikes?

where / nearest beach?

 Weitere Übungen zu „Unit 3, Writing" findest du auf der CD-ROM.

► S. 51

37

thirty-seven

PRACTICE

14 **Read this article about kangaroos** (= *Kängurus*)**. Write the *present passive* form of the verb.**

The kangaroo is one of Australia's favourite animals.

Its picture *is used* (*use*) everywhere: on souvenirs,

on posters and on planes! Wild kangaroos

are found (*find*) all over Australia, not

just in the bush. Red kangaroos live in the centre

of Australia, but grey[1] kangaroos *are seen*

(*see*) in areas where it rains more.

A baby kangaroo *is called* (*call*) a joey

and is only about 2 cm long when it is born.

It *is kept* (*keep*) in its mother's pouch

for about nine months. A joey *is fed* (*feed*)

by its mother for about 18 months.

[1] grey = *grau*

► S. 52

Tip:
present passive =
is/are + past participle

A joey in its mother's pouch

15 **Read this article about a kangaroo hospital.**
Write the *past passive* form of the verb.

Tip:
past passive =
was/were + past participle

Meet Roo. Roo's mother *was killed* (*kill*) by a car, and Roo,

a young joey, *was brought* (*bring*) to the Wilde's

Creek Kangaroo Hospital. Roo *was hurt* (*hurt*) in

the accident, but he *was looked* (*look*) after by the

hospital's vets and now he's fine.

Last year nine kangaroos *were helped* (*help*) at the

hospital. But it nearly had to close because it had money problems. Many people in the

area *were asked* (*ask*) for help. The hospital was lucky: money, equipment and

toys *were sent* (*send*), and the hospital *was saved* (*save*).

► S. 52

Weitere Übungen zu „Unit 3, Practice" findest du auf der CD-ROM.

16 *Going to*-future

a) These people are making New Year's resolutions (= *gute Vorsätze fürs neue Jahr*).
Write the sentences. Use the future with *going to*.

1 I / help my parents more

I'm going to help my

parents more.

2 we / join an art club

We're going to join an art

club.

3 he / eat less chocolate

He's going to eat less

chocolate.

4 they / learn Spanish

They're going to learn

Spanish.

5 she / do her homework
on time

She's going to do her

homework on time.

6 I / go swimming /
more often

I'm going to go swimming

more often.

► S. 82

● **b) Write five New Year's resolutions for yourself.**

17 *Will*-future

James and his friends are organizing a concert.
Write their conversation. Use the *will*-future.

JAMES	*(Who / help me)* phone some bands?
AVA	*(I / help you).*
RUBY	*(I / make)* some posters on my computer.
DAN & AVA	*(We / put)* the posters in all the shops.
JAMES	Ruby, *(you and Luke / make)* some tickets for the concert?
RUBY	Yes, then *(we / take)* them to school and sell them.
JAMES	*(Who / ask)* the teachers if we can use the school gym?
EVERYBODY	Not me!!
JAMES	OK, OK, *(I / do)* it!

► S. 83

Weitere Übungen zu „Revision" findest du auf der CD-ROM.

18 **a) You're going to describe a picture.**
Find other words for the words in blue.

Tip:
If you've forgotten a word, or don't know it, don't panic. Use other words instead.

1 The woman is sitting on the grass. ➔ The woman is sitting on the *ground*.

2 She's listening to her MP3 player. ➔ She's listening to *music*.

3 The boys are laughing. ➔ The boys are enjoying *themselves*.

4 The weather is hot. ➔ The weather is very *warm/nice*.

TP **b) What can you see in the picture?**
Answer all the questions.
Write one sentence or more for each question.

Tip:
Remember the phrases from exercise 2a) on page 31:
in the foreground / on the left, etc.

1 How many people are there and where are they?   *There are twelve / lots of people.*

   They're in a park.

2 What's the woman doing?   *She's listening to her MP3 player and reading a magazine.*

3 Describe the woman.   *She has long black hair and she's wearing shorts. She has*

   sunglasses.

4 What's the little girl doing?   *She's eating an ice cream.*

5 What are the boys doing?   *They're talking and laughing.*

6 What's the weather like?   *It's hot and sunny.*

7 What other things can you see in the picture, and where? (Write two sentences or more.)

   On the right I can see two dogs. They're playing with a ball. In the background

   there's a cafe.

19 a) Give your opinions.
Write six long and interesting sentences.

Tip:
• Use different words and phrases (not always *I like / I don't like*).
• Write longer sentences with *because, and* and *but*.

I love I really like I'm (not) a big fan of I'm (not) very keen on I don't like I hate	sports programmes talk shows news programmes hip-hop music Avril Lavigne Brad Pitt	because and but	I think	they're it's he's she's	awesome • funny boring • terrible interesting • cool
			in my opinion	he's he isn't she's she isn't	a great dancer a good actor good-looking

b) Read Jake's e-mail. Then write an e-mail to him and answer his questions. The sentences in 19a) can help you.

> Hi!
> Many thanks for your e-mail. I'm sending you some photos of the band I'm in.
> What kind of music do you like? Do you like rap? What kind of TV programmes do you like? Who's your favourite star?
> Write soon.
> Jake

20 A school trip to Cairns.
a) Read the start of the story.

Katy lives in Queensland, Australia.

Last week, Katy and her class went with her class to Cairns, on the coast. They went on a boat trip to an island, where they went swimming in the sea and saw lots of beautiful tropical fish. When the boat came back to Cairns, the class went to the Night Markets, a market hall with lots of little souvenir shops. Their coach was in front of the Night Markets.

Katy looked round one shop for a long time, but when she came out, she couldn't see her class or her teacher. She went to the coach, but they weren't there. Oh no! ...

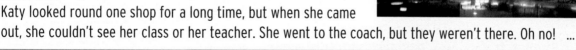

b) Now finish the story in your own words.
These questions can help you:
• Where did Katy look for her class?
• Did she ask some other people?
• How did she feel?
• How long did she look for the others?
• How did she find them?
• What did her teacher say?

Tip:
• Write long sentences with *because, and* and *but*.
• Check your work.
• Correct things that are wrong.

21 **a) These are useful phrases for a letter. Write the missing words.**

1 Dear Sir/*Madam*_____ ,

2 *I'm*_____ writing to ask *for*_____ some information.

3 I'm coming to England *with*_____ my family.

4 *Can/Could*_____ you please send *me/us*_____ some brochures?

5 I'm looking *forward*_____ to hearing from *you*_____ .

6 Yours *faithfully*_____

TP **b) You're going to visit Whitby, a town in the North of England. Write a letter to the tourist office and ask for information.**

Tip:
The phrases in 21a) can help you.

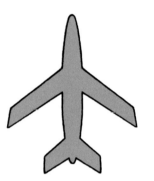

how far /
Teeside airport?

change trains?

nearest
campground?

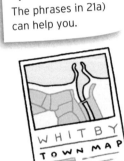

send map of town?

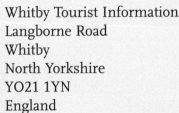

Whitby

Whitby Tourist Information
Langborne Road
Whitby
North Yorkshire
YO21 1YN
England

TP ● **22** **Your English friend, Mel, has sent you this e-mail. Write an e-mail back to Mel. Tell her what you did at the weekend.**

Then after lunch on Sunday, I went to the park with my friend Caroline, who lives in my street. We wanted to play tennis, but it started to rain so we came home.

Tip:
• Think about how to start and end the e-mail. It's to a friend, so don't write *Dear Sir/Madam* and *Yours faithfully*!
• Show that your English is really good!
  – Write longer sentences, with *because, and* and *but*.
  – Use time phrases like *first, then, in the evening* and *after that*.
• Check your work. Correct things that are wrong.

Unit 4
Under pressure?

TP **1** **Listen to the four teenagers again. Are these sentences true (T) or false (F)?**

1 Alex would like to work with dogs and cats. *F*

2 There's lots of unemployment where Alex lives. *T*

3 Ruby has lots of big problems at the moment. *F*

4 Ruby has her own room. *F*

5 Ruby's parents don't always understand her. *T*

6 Zara feels under pressure because she has exams. *T*

7 Zara always gets good marks at school. *F*

8 Lewis has problems with his girlfriend. *T*

▶ S. 55

2 **a) Olivia is under pressure! Write the topics that she's thinking about.**

> alcohol and drugs • family life and parents • girlfriends/boyfriends
> homework • future plans/job • money • taking exams
> problems with other teenagers

1 I don't know what I'll do when I leave school.
I don't know where I want to work.

future plans/job

4 I had a date with a really cool boy. I thought it
was great, but he hasn't phoned me …

girlfriends/boyfriends

2 Our teachers give us too much
to do after school, and it's too
hard. I don't have any time
left for myself!

homework

5 Our teachers give us lots
of tests, and I hate them.
Next month we're having big,
important tests. Oh no!

taking exams

3 People in my class take things from my bag
when I'm not looking. I can't do anything
about it because they're bigger than me.

6 I'm not allowed to come home late and I often
have to look after my little sister. It's not fair!

problems with other teenagers

family life and parents

b) What should Olivia do? Write some advice for three of her problems. ▶ S. 55

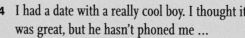

TP **3** **a)** Some teenagers have posted these problems on a website's chat room. Read the answers first. Then read the problems. What was the problem?

Answer	1	2	3	4	5	6
Problem	*D*	*G*	*E*	*A*	*B*	*H*

Tip:
You won't find the same words in the questions and answers. You have to read each answer carefully to find out what it's about.

Answers:

1 Join in with activities, for example join a sports club or, if you like singing, join the school choir. You'll meet lots of people that way, in your own class and other classes too. Remember to smile: if you look friendly, people will talk to you.

2 Write down what you spend. Do you buy things that you don't need? You could tell your parents what you need to buy and ask them for more pocket money – or maybe you should start earning some money yourself.

3 I was just like you till I started doing karate. Don't laugh – it's true! Karate isn't about violence. It gives you more confidence and makes you feel calm and strong. Try it – it'll make you feel good about yourself!

4 Don't do it – you know it isn't fair! Talk to somebody you trust, for example a nice teacher or a relation (an aunt, cousin, grandparent?), and tell them what these people are doing.

5 Before you say anything, help them with the housework for a week! Don't go into town with your friends every evening. Spend more time doing your homework, then ask them to help you!

6 Why don't you phone her or text her? Perhaps there's a good reason, e.g. she's been on holiday, she's ill, or she has a problem. Ask to meet her. If she wants to finish with you, she should tell you to your face.

Problems:

A All my friends bully this new boy in our class. They want me to join in but I feel bad about it. What can I do?

B I've got bad marks in my exams. *Really* bad. How can I tell my parents? They're going to be so angry...

C I don't like my boyfriend. How can I finish with him?

D I've just changed schools. How can I make new friends?

E I'm not very self-confident. Any ideas?

F My teachers are too strict.

G Help! I never have any pocket money left at the end of the week!

H My girlfriend hasn't phoned me for two weeks. What should I do?

b) AND YOU?

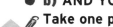

Take one problem (A–H) from page 44 and write your answer.

c) Remember, you can often guess words without using a dictionary.
Find these words from the answers on page 44. Guess their meanings.
How did you guess? Put ticks in the table. (You can put more than one tick.)

English	I know part of the word/ phrase.	I can guess from the context.	It looks like a German word.	German
1 choir (answer 1)		✔	✔	*Chor*
2 karate (answer 3)			✔	*Karate*
3 fair (answer 4)			✔	*fair*
4 relation (answer 4)		✔		*Verwandte/r*
5 housework (answer 5)	✔			*Hausarbeit*

▶ S. 57

4 **a) What to do if people are bullying you ...**
Read the sentences. What goes together? Write the letters (a–h).

1 = *c*   2 = *f*   3 = *d*   4 = *a*   5 = *h*   6 = *b*   7 = *e*   8 = *g*

1 Don't just hope the bullying will stop – do ...
2 For example, talk to somebody you can trust, like ...
3 Ask a friend to walk to school with you so you're ...
4 If you find it hard to talk to somebody, ...
5 In school, stay in a safe area where there are ...
6 Don't fight back, even if the bullies use violence – ...
7 Keep unkind e-mails and text messages, ...
8 Remember – nobody has the right to ...

a write them a note instead.
b you could get hurt.
c something to make it stop!
d not alone.
e and show them to a teacher.
f a teacher, a counsellor or a relation.
g bully you!
h lots of other people.

b) Now write the sentences together to make an article.

What to do if people are bullying you ...
Don't just hope that the bullying will
stop – do something to make it stop!
For example, talk to ...

45

forty-five

▶ S. 57

WRITING

5 Write these sentences in your exercise book. Put them together with *because, and* or *but*. This shows that your English is really good.

1 In my opinion, tattoos look terrible. **?** They're expensive too.

In my opinion, tattoos look terrible and they're expensive too.

2 I wouldn't like to have a tattoo. **?** I think they look good on other people.   *(but)*

3 I can't have a tattoo. **?** My parents say I'm too young.   *(because)*

4 I don't like tattoos. **?** My friends hate them too.   *(and)*

5 On the one hand, I'd like to have a tattoo now. **?**

On the other hand, perhaps I won't like it when I'm 90!   *(but)*

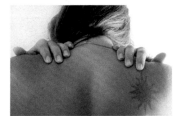

6 I think tattoos are cool. **?** They make you look different from other people too.   *(and)*

7 I'd like to get a tattoo. **?** I won't. **?** They hurt when you get them.   *(but) (because)*

▸ S. 59

6 a) Copy the mind map about tattoos and finish it. Use your own ideas.

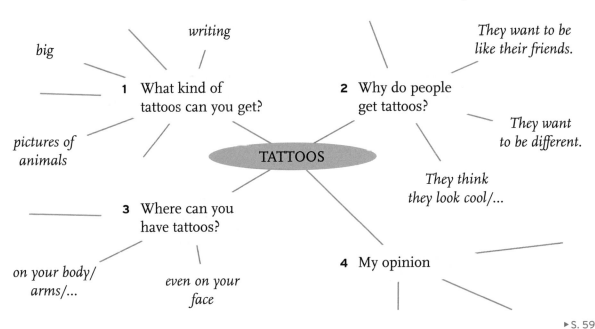

▸ S. 59

b) Now look at the checklist to help you plan and write a text about tattoos.
- **Think of a title.**
- **Write your text. The ideas from the mind map in exercise 6a) can help you.**
- **Check your text. Use the checklist again.**
- **Correct mistakes, or write your text again to make it better.**

Checklist:
- Does the text have a good title?
- Is the spelling right? Use a dictionary.
- Is the word order right?
- Does each paragraph have one main point?
- Are there lots of different verbs?
- Are the verbs in the right tense?
- Are there words like *and, but, because, also, ...*?

Weitere Übungen zu „Unit 4, Writing" findest du auf der CD-ROM.

TP 7 **Look at each picture and listen to the three sentences.**
Which sentence best describes the picture? Tick A, B or C.

○ 24

1 A ☐ B ☐ C ✔

2 A ✔ B ☐ C ☐

3 A ☐ B ✔ C ☐

4 A ☐ B ☐ C ✔

¹ swot = *Streberin*

▶ S. 60

TP 8 **Listen to the phone calls.**
Complete these phone messages.

○ 25

> **Tip:**
> • Listen carefully and then write your answers quickly.
> • When you've stopped listening, check your English.
>   Are there any mistakes?

1 ☎ *From:* Peter

Message: He can't come to *the concert*

on *Thursday* because he has

an exam on *Friday*.

2 ☎ *From:* Mandy

Message: She can go to *the party*

with Rob on *Saturday*, but she has

to *be home at 11 p.m*.

3 ☎ *From:* Rachel

Message: Do you want to *go out at the*

weekend? Phone her *this*

evening.

4 ☎ *From:* Tom

Message: *Meet him/Tom after school*

tomorrow. Bring your MP3 player.

▶ S. 60

○ Weitere Übungen zu „Unit 4, Listening" findest du auf der CD-ROM.

9 **WORDPOWER**
a) Jobs at home. Fill in the right verbs.

	clean my bedroom.
never	_lay_ the table.
don't	_empty_ the dishwasher.
I sometimes	_take out_ the rubbish.
often	_cook_ meals.
always	_fix_ the computer when it doesn't work.

b) How often do you do these six things at home? Write sentences with *and*, *but* and *too*.

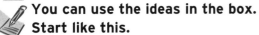
I often lay the table and I sometimes cook meals too.

48

forty-eight

● **c) ROLE PLAY**
Make a survey form. Use the ideas in exercise 9a).
Then ask five people these questions and tick their answers on the survey form.

Survey: jobs you do at home				
	always	often	sometimes	never
How often do you clean your bedroom?		✔	✔ ✔ ✔	✔
How often do you lay the table?	✔ ✔	✔ ✔		✔
How often do you ...				

▶ S. 62

● **10** **a)** Write this conversation between a teenage girl and her mother.
You can use the ideas in the box.
Start like this.

MOTHER What's wrong?

GIRL You know what's wrong. I ...

MOTHER ...

Ideas:

girl: live my life • have more freedom • go out
make my own decisions • too strict

mum: responsible for • still young • make mistakes
worry about you • dangerous

b) Act your conversation with your partner.

▶ S. 62

TP **11** INTERPRETING

You and your friend, Julia, are staying with an Irish friend, Ryan. Julia's English isn't very good, so you interpret for her.

Tip:
Use the right pronouns.
I have to be ... → Er muss ...

JULIA Sind deine Eltern streng, Ryan?

YOU Are your *parents strict, Ryan?*

RYAN Yes, very. I have to be home before 9.30 p.m.

YOU *Ja, sehr. Er muss vor halb zehn zu Hause sein.*

JULIA Sogar am Wochenende? Das ist nicht fair!

YOU *Even at the weekend? That isn't fair!*

RYAN I'm allowed to stay out a bit later at the weekend. What about you?

YOU *Er darf am Wochenende ein bisschen länger ausbleiben. Wie ist es bei dir?*

JULIA Meine Eltern sind nicht zu streng, aber ich muss sie anrufen, wenn es ein Problem gibt.

YOU *Her parents aren't too strict, but she has to phone them if there's a problem.*

►S. 63

TP **12** MEDIATING

Fathers and sons
Tell your partner the joke in German.

Tip:
You don't have to translate every word.
You can change the words a bit.

*A father is reading his newspaper one day.
His young son comes in and asks, "Dad, will
you take me to the zoo tomorrow?"
"No," says his dad. "If they want you, they
can come and get you."*

►S. 63

PRACTICE

13 **Questions for Mum.**
Circle the right word: *do, does* **or** *did.*

1 *Do / Does / Did* you have £9 for my school dinners this week?

2 Where *do / does / did* you put my trainers?

3 *Do / Does / Did* I have to go to school today?

4 *Do / Does / Did* you buy some milk yesterday?

5 How *do / does / did* the dishwasher work?

▶ S. 66

14 **Questions about last night. Two friends are talking.**
Finish this conversation and write the questions.

1 | last | you | where | go | did | night | ? |
Where did you go last night?

– I went to a party.

2 | go | did | who | with | you | ? |
Who did you go with?

– I went with my friend.

3 | you | how | did | get | home | ? |
How did you get home?

– We walked home.

4 | party | finish | the | did | when | ? |
When did the party finish?

– It finished at 1 a.m. and I got home at 1.30 a.m.

5 | did | say | your | what | parents | ? |
What did your parents say?

– They were really angry! They said I can't go to any parties for two months!

▶ S. 66

15 **AND YOU?**
Questions for a star.
Write five questions
(● ten questions) you'd like to
ask your favourite celebrity.

When did you ...?

Ideas:
• when / start singing / playing football / ...?
• where / live?
• what / do in your free time?
• your family come to all your concerts/matches/...?
• like German music?

▶ S. 66

Weitere Übungen zu „Unit 4, Practice" findest du auf der CD-ROM.

16 *ing*-form

a) What's your opinion about these things? Write six sentences in your exercise book.

Doing homework		fun boring important awesome
Watching *Formula 1* racing		
Eating lots of fast food	is ...	exciting dangerous great interesting
Going shopping in town		expensive hard good/bad for you
Playing cards		
Learning another language		useful a waste of time nice terrible
Chatting online		

b) Write your opinion about six other things. For example: concerts, sports, food, hobbies or things you have to do at home or at school.

Going to concerts is ... / Doing ... / Eating ...

▶S. 88

17 Complete this postcard. Fill in the right verbs in the *ing*-form.

→ dive • have • rain • read • see • show • sit • swim

Hi Pete,

I'm having a great holiday! I went <u>swimming</u>  every day last week,

and on Friday I tried <u>diving</u> , which was awesome!

The weather isn't very good at the moment, but when it stops <u>raining</u>

we'll go to the beach. My sister likes <u>reading</u> books in the sun,

but I hate <u>sitting</u> on the beach doing nothing – it's just boring!

Tomorrow I'm going to start my <u>surfing</u> lessons.

That should be fun!

I'm looking forward to <u>seeing</u>   you soon and <u>showing</u>

you my photos!

Tim

Weitere Übungen zu „Revision" findest du auf der CD-ROM.

▶S. 88

TP **18** **Listen and write the prices (1–4) and the times (5–8).**

How much?
⊙ 26

1 £ 21.50

2 £ 4.60

3 £ 18

4 £ 1.40

What time?

5   6   7   8

---

19 **a) Find words and phrases that mean the same kind of thing. Write the letters:**

A + E	B + J	C + N	D + K
F + M	G + O	H + P	I + L

A my parents   **B** music   **C** riding my bike   **D** at home

E mum and dad   **F** cinema   **G** reading   **H** great   **I** a week

J my MP3 player   **K** at my house   **L** seven days   **M** films

N cycling   **O** books and magazines   **P** awesome

TP **19** **b) Now listen. Which hobbies does each person have?**
⊙ 27 **Look at the pictures and write the letters.**

1 Fiona's hobbies: C + E

2 Mark's hobbies: A + D

3 Jenny's hobbies: B + G

4 Adam's hobbies: F + H

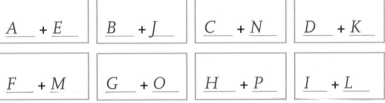

A music   B pets   C films   D reading

E cycling

F sport   G shopping

H going out with the family

TP **20** Jake is talking to a friend about helping at home.
Are these sentences true?
Tick *true* or *false*.

◉ 28

Tip:
Listen carefully –
small words can
change the meaning!
For example:
I never cook and clean
is the opposite of
I often cook and clean.

	true	false
1 Jake helps his parents at home.	✔	
2 He lays the table.		✔
3 He empties the dishwasher.	✔	
4 Jake's sister helps their parents too.		✔
5 Jake thinks it's fair that children help at home.		✔

TP **21** Lydia has a job interview.

◉ 29　Sentences 1–5: tick A, B, or C.

Tip:
Read the questions before you listen.
Then you'll know:
– what the text is about.
– what information you need to find.

● Questions 6–8: write the answers.

1 Lydia wants a job …

A ✔ in a department store.　B ☐ in a cafe.　C ☐ in a hotel.

2 She had a job …

A ☐ last month.　B ☐ last winter.　C ✔ last summer.

3 Lydia's hobby is …

A ☐ sport.　B ✔ music.　C ☐ cooking.

4 Lydia could work on …

A ☐ Saturdays only.　B ✔ Saturdays and Thursday evenings.

C ☐ Saturday evenings and Thursday evenings.

5 She could start work …

A ☐ next Saturday.　B ☐ next Thursday.　C ✔ on Saturday 18th.

● 6 When will Lydia start and finish work on a Saturday?

She'll start at 10 a.m. and finish at 4.30 p.m.

● 7 What will she have to wear?

She'll have to wear a blue and white uniform.

● 8 How much will Lydia earn when she starts?

She'll earn £4.20 per hour.

EXAM TIPS

1 **Look at the pictures and read the tips on pages 54 and 55.
Find the right tip for each picture.**

Preparing for the exam ...

Tip *C*

Tip *G*

Tip *D*

Tip *F*

A Check the date and time of the exam.
Don't arrive late!

B Don't forget your pens, pencils, ruler
and dictionary when you go to the exam.
Take at least two pens!

C Work every day for a short time.
And make a plan of what you're going
to do each day.

D Work where it's quiet, for example
in the library. Don't watch TV while
you're trying to prepare for your exam.

Tip _A_

Tip _H_

Tip _B_

Tip _E_

E Don't panic in the exam! Read the questions slowly and carefully – and do your best!

G Learn the things you find most difficult, not the easy things that you know! Write notes to help you learn them. If you don't understand something, ask a friend or your teacher.

F Work hard, but do some sport or other exercise too. Working all the time isn't good for you!

H Have a good breakfast on the morning of the exam. It'll help you to think well, and you won't feel hungry while you work.

EXAM TIPS

2 **Tips for your exam! Finish the sentences.**

→ at the end. • go to the next question. • no mark! • the example answer.
time do you have? • verb tenses, spelling, word order.

1 Before you start, check – how many questions are there?

How much *time do you have?* _____

2 Read each question carefully and look at *the example answer.* _____

3 Leave time to check your answers *at the end.* _____

4 In the writing exam, think about things to check, for example:

verb tenses, spelling, word order. _____

5 If a question is very hard, don't panic! Try to answer (or guess!),

then *go to the next question.* _____

6 Answer all the questions because no answer means *no mark!* _____

3 **You also know tips for *Speaking, Reading, Writing* and *Listening*!
Look at the Portfolio pages 28 and 30. Write two tips for each – in German:**

Speaking Tips

_____
_____
_____
_____

Reading Tips

_____
_____
_____
_____

Writing Tips

_____
_____
_____

Listening Tips

_____
_____
_____